27 Character Traits of the New Testament:

Stories & Activities for Children

Matthew - Revelation

27 Character Traits of the New Testament:
Stories & Activities for Children
Matthew - Revelation

By: Jean Ann Williams

Illustrated by Carley Herlihy

Reading Ease: Grade 1 & Younger

How to Use this Book

Please read the Bible verses referenced at the beginning of each story with your child. The Scriptures could be part of family devotions, a lesson, or simply shared in order to give the child a background they will need to successfully guess the riddles in this book. Then allow your young reader the opportunity to read to you from this volume and solve the puzzles. This book is designed to be done over time and not in one sitting. Please enjoy this adventure through the New Testament.

Jean Ann Williams

Dedication:

To the children who have been rescued from human traffickers: It is my prayer each little one will learn about our Father in Heaven and the characters written about in God's Word. People around the world are praying for you!

Note to Parents:

The story of Thankful is based on fact. I took the liberty to add how the crowd may have felt. All other biblical accounts had enough information on its own to show children how God used people and His Son to carry out His plans.

Listening ~ Luke 1: 5-24, 57-76

Riddle: I was not able to talk. My listening turned into faith. Who am I?

My Story: I was doing my job in the temple. An angel stood near me. I was afraid.

The angel told me to not be afraid. He said God heard my prayer for a child.

My wife will give birth to a son. I said, "How shall I know this?" I was an old man.

My wife was an old woman. The angel said God sent him to me.

He told me this good news. I doubted him. I talked no more. I will talk when our son is born.

1

Listening ~ Luke 1: 5-24, 57-76

Bonus: Name my son.

Months passed. The day came when our son was born. Our family and friends were happy. They wanted to call him by my name. I waved my hands. I needed to write on a paper. I wrote down his name. My tongue worked again. I talked.

I talked about our son. Our son will become a prophet of the Lord. He will tell people about the Lord's plan. God blessed me. Words from my faith came true. Our son grew up. He told of the coming of the Lord.

2

Listening Puzzle Clues

Across

2. He will tell people about the Lord's _____. (4)

4. My listening turned into _____. (5)

5. My _____ worked again. (6)

6. I _____ no more. (6)

Down

1. Who am I? (9)

3. Our son will become a _____ of the Lord. (7)

Listening Puzzle Grid

4

Joyful ~ Luke 1:5-17, 24, 25, 39-44, 57-63

Riddle: I was old. I had no child. Then, I had a child. Who am I?

My Story: My husband had a job at the temple. One day he came home from his job. He opened his mouth. But he could not speak. He wrote on paper. It said that an angel came to him. The angel said I was to have a son. He named our son. Joy came into my heart.

One day my cousin came to see me. The baby inside my belly moved in joy. I told my cousin she was blessed of all women. She was the mother of my Lord.

5

Joyful ~ Luke 1:5-17, 24, 25, 39-44, 57-63

Bonus: Name my husband.

One day our son was born. People were happy. I had a boy. I told the people what we named him. They said, "None of your kin have this name."

My husband took paper. He wrote down our son's name. Now my husband talked.

"Our son will grow up. He will tell people about the Lord. Then the Lord will come. The Lord will talk to the people. Many will have joy."

Joyful Puzzle Clues

Across

1. I told my cousin she was _____ of all women. (7)

3. Name my son. (4)

4. Name my cousin. (4)

Down

2. The angel said I was to have a _____. (3)

3. _____ came into my heart. (3)

Joyful Puzzle Grid

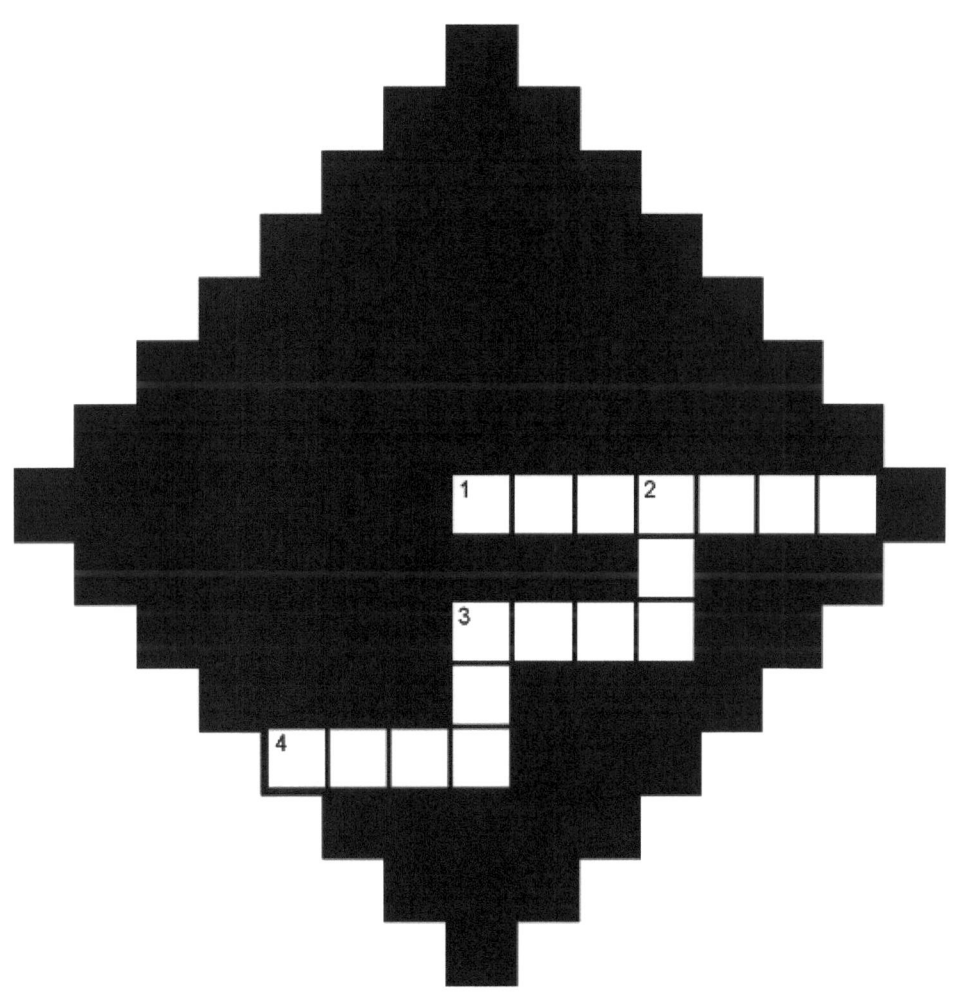

Favored ~ Luke 1:26-49

Riddle: I was a young woman. An angel came to me with good news. Who am I?

My Story: An angel woke me. The angel said I was favored. God was with me.

I wanted to know more. The angel told me to not fear. He said a child will grow inside me. He is the Christ. The child is holy. His kingdom will have no end.

I was unsure. The angel said the Holy Ghost will come. The power of God will cover me. The child will be called the Son of God.

9

Favored ~ Luke 1:26-49

Bonus: Name the angel.

The angel talked of my older cousin. She will also have a son. God can do all things.

I said, "I am the server of the Lord. Let it be as you say."

The angel left. I went to see my cousin. She said she was to have a son. Just as the angel had said.

My heart beat with joy. I sang. I was favored by the Lord.

All peoples will call me blessed.

Favored Puzzle Clues

Across

3. Name the child. (6)

6. Name the angel. (7)

Down

1. The angel said I was _____. (7)

2. My _____ beat with joy. (5)

4. The child is _____. (4)

5. I am the _____ of the Lord. (6)

Favored Puzzle Grid

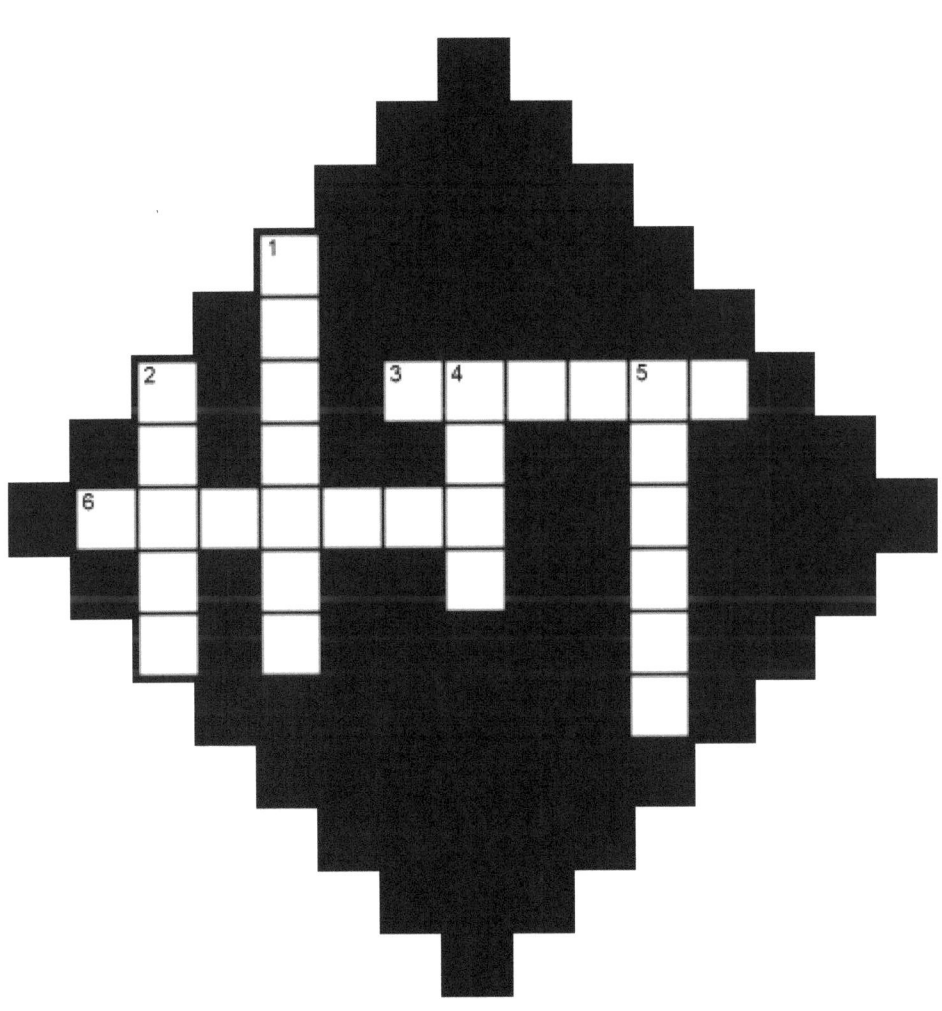

Obeying ~ Matthew 1:18-25; 2:11-13; Luke 2:1-16

Riddle: An angel of the Lord came to me. Who am I?

My Story: An angel spoke to me while I slept. He said to take a wife. She was to have a child from the Holy Ghost. I married her. We went to a town. We stayed in a stinky barn. She gave birth to God's Son.

She wrapped him in cloth. She laid him in an animal feed bin. Wise men saw Christ's star. They knew the star shined over God's Son. They came to meet him. They fell down to worship the child. They gave him gifts.

13

Obeying ~ Matthew 1:18-25; 2:11-13; Luke 2:1-16

Bonus: Name how many times the angel came.

The angel came to me as I slept. He told me to run to a safe place. Not to go back home. A bad man wanted to kill the child. So we left. Then the angel came to me again. He said to take the child and my wife. Go to Israel. The bad man had died.

I rose in a hurry. But the bad man's son now ruled. The angel told us to go to a small town in Israel. We stayed there as the Son grew into a man. I was an obeying man. I saved the Christ. Then he saved people from their sins.

Obeying Puzzle Clues

Across

3. Name the last place I took my family. (8)

5. They gave him _____. (5)

Down

1. Name how many times the angel came. (4)

2. Name my wife. (4)

4. Who came to me while I slept? (5)

6. Wise men saw Christ's _____. (4)

Obeying Puzzle Grid

Self-Control ~ Matthew 3:1-6, 11, 12, 13-17

Riddle: I wore animal hair for clothes. Who am I?

My Story: I was born for this day. I went into the river. I called for the people to tell their sins. I said, "Listen. The kingdom of heaven is near." People were sorry for their sins. I dunked them in the water. They came back up. This is how they were baptized.

I said a great man will come. I am not great, not even to touch his shoes. He will baptize people in the Holy Ghost and fire.

Self-Control ~ Matthew 3:1-6, 11, 12, 13-17

Bonus: Name the animal hair I wore.

The man came to me. He asked me to baptize him. I said I needed him to baptize me. He said for me to do this. To show all truth. I dunked him into the river. He came back up.

The heavens opened. A bird flew down. The bird rested on him. A voice came from heaven. "This is my much loved Son. I am well pleased with him."

I was glad. I had self-control. Now the people knew about this great man.

Self-Control Puzzle Clues

Across

3. Name the animal hair I wore. (5)

4. Who am I? (4)

5. This is how they were _____. (8)

Down

1. Name the river where I baptized the people. (6)

2. Name the bird that flew down from Heaven. (4)

3. Who wanted me to baptize him? (6)

Self-Control Puzzle Grid

Patient ~ Luke 2:22-35

Riddle: I loved God. I will see the Lord's Christ. Who am I?

My Story: All first born boys went to the temple. Their parents showed them to the Lord there. These boys were holy to the Lord. This was God's law.

The parents gave a gift. They gave two doves or pigeons. I was patient a long time.

I waited for the joy of our people. The Lord said it was worth the wait.

Patient ~ Luke 2:22-35

Bonus: Name the city.

The Spirit told me to go to the temple. The Christ child came with his parents. I took him in my arms. I blessed God. I now had peace. My eyes had seen the Lord's salvation. This was a light to others. A glory to the Lord's people. I blessed his mom and dad.

I said to his mom, "This child is set for the fall and the rise again of many in Israel. Your own soul will hurt. What people think in their hearts will be shown." I was glad I was patient. I saw the Lord's Christ.

Patient Puzzle Clues

Across

1. I saw the Lord's _____. (6)

3. The parents gave a _____. (4)

5. I _____ God. (7)

6. I was glad I was _____. (7)

Down

2. Who am I? (6)

4. The Spirit told me to go to the _____. (6)

Patient Puzzle Grid

Faithful ~ Matthew 4:1-11

Riddle: The Lord sent me to a quiet place. The evil one tempted me. Who am I?

My Story: I did not eat for days. The evil one said, "If you are the Son of God make the rocks into bread."

I said, "Man shall not live only by bread. Man lives by the words from God." The evil one set me on the temple. He said, "If you are the Son of God fall down. God will send angels to save you. The angels will hold you up. You will not be hurt."

25

Faithful ~ Matthew 4:1-11

Bonus: Name the evil one.

I said that no one shall tempt the Lord. The evil one took me high up. He showed me kingdoms. The kingdoms were nice. He will give these to me. But I must fall down to worship him. I said, "Get behind me evil one. We worship God only. We serve Him."

The evil one ran away. I needed to eat. Angels came. They took care of me.

I stayed faithful even from the evil one. I showed people they can trust in me.

Faithful Puzzle Clues

Across

2. Who took care of me? (6)

4. Name the quiet place the Lord had sent me. (10)

6. I stayed _____ even from the evil one. (8)

Down

1. Name the evil one. (5)

3. We worship _____ only. (3)

5. I needed to _____. (3)

Faithful Puzzle Grid

Perfect Love ~ Mark 10:1, 10, 13-16; Matthew 18:4-6

Riddle: Children came to me. Who am I?

My Story: My men and I walked a long way. We came to the coast. We went into a house to rest.

People brought young children. They wanted me to see their children. They wanted me to bless them. My men said no. My men stood in the people's way. They did not let the children inside.

I saw what happened. I was not happy with my men.

29

Perfect Love ~ Mark 10:1, 10, 13-16; Matthew 18:4-6

Bonus: Name what my men are called.

I told the truth to my men. "Let the little children come. Do not keep them from me. Little children are in the kingdom of God."

My men had to change their hearts. They needed to become like little children. Or they will not be in the kingdom of heaven.

Now I took the little children in my arms. I lay my hands on them. I blessed them. I had perfect love. I came to save the world from sin.

Perfect Love Puzzle Clues

Across

3. Who am I? (6)

5. Little children are in the _____ of God. (7)

6. I had perfect _____. (4)

Down

1. Name what my men are called. (9)

2. Who came to me? (8)

4. I told the _____ to my men. (5)

Perfect Love Puzzle Grid

Thankful ~ Matthew 21:1-11

Riddle: We showed respect to Christ. We know he is King. Who are we?

Our Story: Our Lord said for two of his men to get animals. One was the mother. One was the baby. He said the Lord needs them.

This was all done from what a wise man once said. "Your King comes to you. He is meek. He sits on the animal."

The men got the animals. They put clothes on their backs. They sat Christ down. He rode away.

33

Thankful ~ Matthew 21:1-11

Bonus: Name the place Christ came to.

Then we laid our clothes on the road. Others cut limbs from trees. We laid them down.

Christ rode over them. We walked with him. We were all around him.

We were thankful. We said he was great. He was blessed. Christ came in the name of the Lord. He was above all people. Christ came to the place. The people there said, "Who is this man?" We said he is the prophet of the Lord.

We saw the Christ. We got to tell the people about God's Son.

Thankful Puzzle Clues

Across

3. Your _____ comes to you. (4)

4. Name the place Christ came to. (9)

6. Who are we? (5)

Down

1. Name the animal Christ rode on. (6)

2. Others cut _____ from trees. (5)

5. Christ came in the name of the _____. (4)

Thankful Puzzle Grid

Discernment ~ John 2:13-16

Riddle: I rode on a donkey. But now I was angry. Who am I?

My Story: I went to my Father's house. Men there sold animals. This was bad. I had to teach them a lesson.

My Father did not like this. I told people they were bad. Now I had a job to do.

I wove small ropes into one. The ropes were in my fist. I did not plan to hurt the men. I did not plan to hurt the animals.

Discernment ~ John 2:13-16

Bonus: Name the Father's house.

I swung the ropes. I had to make the men leave. They ran away with their animals. I poured out the money box. Then I pushed over the tables. One by one I pushed them over. I spoke to men who sold doves.

"Take these things out. And do not do this in my Father's house. Do not sell here. My Father's house is not a store."

I had discernment. I knew God's ways. I came to this world for good. But I had to show the evil too.

Discernment Puzzle Clues

Across

2. Who am I? (6)

4. But now I was _____. (5)

6. But I had to show the ____ too. (4)

Down

1. Men there sold _____. (7)

3. Name the Father's house. (6)

5. I came to this world for _____. (4)

Discernment Puzzle Grid

Honesty ~ John 4:6-30, 39-41

Riddle: A man told me about water. Who am I?

My Story: I came to get water at a well. A man said, "Give me a drink."

I said, "How is it that you, a Jew, ask me for a drink? The Jews do not like my people."

He asked if I knew God's gift. He said, "I give living water."

I said, "Sir, where do you get this water?" He said we drink well water. We will need more. Those who drink of the water he gives will never need more.

41

Honesty ~ John 4:6-30, 39-41

Bonus: Name my city.

The water he gives is life. "Sir, give me this water." Then the man told me things I had done. I said he was wise. I knew Christ was coming. He will tell us all things.

The man said, "I am he."

I left my waterpot. I ran to town. "Come. See a man. Can this be the Christ?" People went to the well. Christ stayed with us for two days. Many people believed his words. I was glad. I had honesty. I told the truth about him.

Honesty Puzzle Clues

Across

2. Then the man told me things I had _____. (4)

3. I said he was _____. (4)

4. He asked if I knew of God's _____. (4)

Down

1. I had _____. (7)

3. I left my _____. (8)

Honesty Puzzle Grid

Sharing Lad ~ John 6:1-14

Riddle: I had some food. A great man made more. Who am I?

My Story: I walked in a crowd. We followed a great man. We went up a hill. I hung on to my basket of bread and fish. We came to the top. The great man asked where to buy bread. He did not want the people to faint from hunger. I stared at my basket.

Someone said I had five small breads and two fish. I was not able to feed the crowd. But I wanted to share. I set my food at the great man's feet.

Sharing Lad ~ John 6:1-14

Bonus: Name the great man.

His men told the crowd to sit on the grass. The great man thanked God for the food. Then he took the bread and the fish from my basket. He passed the food to his men. They gave the food to the crowd.

My basket stayed full of fish and bread. The great man made more. The people ate and ate. The great man told his men to get the food left over. He did not want any waste. They filled twelve baskets with the bread and fish.

I was a sharing lad. God blessed me. I helped to feed the people.

46

Sharing Lad Puzzle Clues

Across

2. He did not want the people to _____ from hunger. (5)

5. I stared at my _____. (6)

6. Who am I? (3)

Down

1. Name the great man. (6)

3. They filled _____ baskets with the bread and fish. (6)

4. I helped to _____ the people. (4)

Sharing Lad Puzzle Grid

Generous Stranger ~ Luke 10:25-37

Riddle: Christ spoke of love. He told a story about me. Who am I?

My Story: Christ said we were to love our neighbors. A man was not sure. Who was his neighbor? Christ began the story of me.

A man walked on a road. Bad men came. They beat the poor man. They stole from him. They left him to die on the road. A priest saw the poor man. He walked away. One more man came by. He saw the poor man's body. He left him there.

I was the next person. I was a stranger to the poor man. That did not matter.

49

Generous Stranger ~ Luke 10:25-37

Bonus: Name the town the poor man walked to.

I was sad for the poor man. I washed his sores. I put cloth on them. I set the man on my beast. Soon I took care of the man in a rented room.

The man was still alive when the sun came up. I gave the keeper of the room money. I paid him to take care of the poor man. I told the keeper I will pay him more if need be.

Christ was done with the story. He said for the man to do as I had done. I did well. I was a generous stranger. I gave help to the poor man.

Generous Stranger Puzzle Clues

Across

1. I gave the keeper of the room _____. (5)

3. A _____ saw the poor man. (6)

4. Name the town the poor man walked to _____. (7)

5. I was a _____ stranger. (8)

6. I was _____ for the poor man. (3)

Down

2. Christ said we were to love our _____. (9)

Generous Stranger Puzzle Grid

Devotion ~ Luke 10:38-42

Riddle: I sat at Christ's feet. My sister did not. Who am I?

My Story: Christ and his men came to our town. My sister told them to come into our house. So they came.

Christ's words gave me hope. My sister did not hear his words. She cooked the food. She fed Christ and his men.

My sister was upset. She wanted me to help. She did not want to feed them alone. It was too much work. Did my sister not want me to hear Christ's words?

53

Devotion ~ Luke 10:38-42

Bonus: Name my sister.

My sister told Christ to make me help.

He said my sister's name. He said it again. Christ said she was sad about many things. He said there was only one good thing. He said I chose the good. It cannot be taken from me.

I showed the world. I chose devotion to Christ. I put him first. It made me glad.

Devotion Puzzle Clues

Across

3. Who am I? (4)

4. I sat at _____ feet. (6)

5. He said I chose the _____. (4)

Down

1. Name my sister. (6)

2. I chose _____ to Christ. (8)

Devotion Puzzle Grid

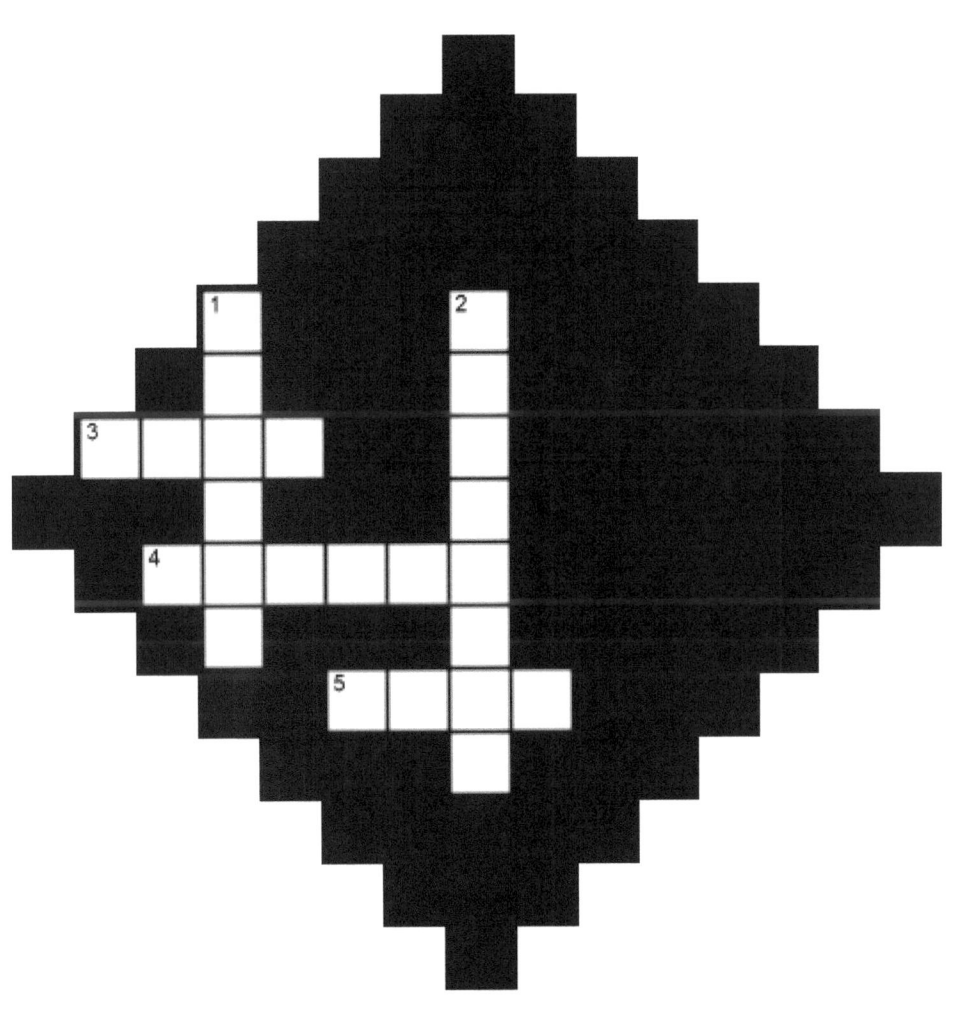

Truth Teller ~ John 9:1-38

Riddle: It was the day of rest. Christ healed my eyes. Who am I?

My Story: Men who smelled of fish passed by me. One man stopped. He spoke. "I am the light of the world." He spit on the dirt. He made mud. He put the mud on my blind eyes. The man said, "Go wash in the pool." I washed. Now I see.

I was brought to the rulers. I told them what the prophet had done. Some rulers said, "This man is not from God. He does not keep the day of rest." Others said this man was a sinner. They wanted to know what I thought of him.

57

Truth Teller ~ John 9:1-38

Bonus: Name the pool.

I believed he was a prophet. I did not know if he was a sinner. But I did know one thing. I was blind. Now I see. The rulers tossed me out on the street. The prophet found me. He said, "Do you believe in the Son of Man?"

"Who is he that I may believe in him?"

"You have seen him. It is he who is speaking to you." I bowed my face before him. "Lord, I believe." I was a truth teller. I made people think. God blessed me. I met God's Son.

Truth Teller Puzzle Clues

Across

3. Name the pool. (6)

4. I met God's _____. (3)

5. Christ healed my _____. (4)

Down

1. I _____ my face before him. (5)

2. Men who smelled of _____ passed by me. (4)

3. Others said this man was a _____. (6)

Truth Teller Puzzle Grid

Vow Keeper ~ Luke 19:1-9

Riddle: I was too short. I went up a tree. Who am I?

My Story: No one liked me. I was top boss of people who took the tax money. I was a rich man. Christ came to my town. People were there to see him. But I was not able to see him.

I ran in front of Christ. I went up a tree. I waited for him to come. He came to my tree. Christ looked up.

He called me by name. "Hurry. Come down. I must stay at your house."

61

Vow Keeper ~ Luke 19:1-9

Bonus: Name the tree I stood in.

I went down fast. Christ wanted to stay at my house! People did not like that. They said he cannot be with a sinner. I vowed this to Christ. "I will give half of my goods to the poor. If I have cheated anyone, I will return it plus four times more."

Christ spoke. "Today salvation has come to this house. For the Son of Man came to seek. He came to save which was lost."

I made a vow to God. Now Christ vowed my salvation. God blessed me.

Vow Keeper Puzzle Clues

Across

2. I must stay at your _____. (5)

4. They said he cannot be with a _____. (6)

5. I made a _____ to God. (3)

Down

1. Who am I? (9)

3. Name the tree I stood in. (8)

4. I was too _____. (5)

Vow Keeper Puzzle Grid

Believing Women ~ John 11:1-5, 11-14, 20-35, 38-44

Riddle: Our brother was sick. We knew Christ can help. Who are we?

Our Story: We did not want our brother to die. We said for Christ to come. We waited. But he did not come. Our brother died. I met Christ on the road. I said much to him. If only he had been there. Now our brother was dead. But God will give Christ what he asks. Christ said our brother will wake.

I ran home to my sister. I told her what he said. She met him on the road. My sister fell at his feet. She cried. Everyone cried. Christ cried too.

65

Believing Women ~ John 11:1-5, 11-14, 20-35, 38-44

Bonus: Name our brother.

Our brother lay inside a cave. Christ said for people to open the stone door. They did as he said. Our brother had been dead four days. My sister said he must stink. Christ told her to believe. This is the time she will see the glory of God. She said she believed.

Christ raised his eyes. He thanked God. God heard him. Christ said for our brother to come. Our brother came. Now our brother was not dead.

We sisters were blessed. Our brother was blessed. Other people believed too.

Believing Women Puzzle Clues

Across

4. Name our brother. (7)

5. Our _____ was sick. (7)

6. My sister fell at his _____. (4)

Down

1. I met _____ on the road. (6)

2. Other people _____ too. (8)

3. Now our brother was not _____. (4)

Believing Women Puzzle Grid

Compassion ~ John 11:1-27, 38-44

Riddle: I loved my friends. And they needed me. Who am I?

My Story: My friend Lazarus was sick. I said, "This sickness is not to the death. This sickness is for the glory of God." So I did not go to my friends for two days. Then I told my men it was time to go. My men were afraid. It was not safe for me. The rulers wanted to stone me. I told my men that I had to go.

I said, "Lazarus is dead. I am glad I was not there for your sakes. Now you will believe."

Martha met us on the road. She said if I asked God anything He would give it.

69

Compassion ~ John 11:1-27, 38-44

Bonus: Name the town I went to.

I said, "Your brother shall rise again. Those who believe in me shall never die. Do you believe this?" She said yes. I came to the cave where Lazarus lay. I groaned. The stone door was open.

I prayed to God, "Father, I thank You. You have heard me. I knew that You always hear me. I said it so people may believe You sent me."

I said in a loud voice, "Lazarus, come here." And he came. I showed compassion. My caring let people know who I am. I did it for the glory of God.

Compassion Puzzle Clues

Across

3. I showed _____. (10)

4. Name the town I went to. (7)

5. My men were _____. (6)

Down

1. This sickness is for the _____ of God. (5)

2. _____ met us on the road. (6)

3. I came to the _____ where Lazarus lay. (4)

Compassion Puzzle Grid

Comforter ~ John 12:1-9

Riddle: I sat at Christ's feet. I held a bottle of oil. Who am I?

My Story: Christ came to our home. It was good to see him. We made food. My brother sat at the table with him.

I loved Christ. I knew what was to come for him. I wanted to be a comforter.

I came to where he sat at the table. I had my bottle of sweet smelling oil. The oil was worth a lot of money. I sat at his feet. I poured the oil on his feet. I wiped his feet with my long hair. Our home smelled of the oil.

Comforter ~ John 12:1-9

Bonus: Name the man who wanted to sell my oil.

One of Christ's men was upset. He did not want me to use the oil in this way. He wanted to sell the oil. He wanted to give the money to the poor.

Christ said to the man, "Let her be. She is making me ready for my burial. You will have the poor. Soon you will not have me."

I was glad I was a comforter. Christ was blessed by my care for him. And Christ blessed me too.

Comforter Puzzle Clues

Across

2. She is making me ready for my _____. (6)

3. Name the man who wanted to sell my oil. (5)

5. I wanted to be a _____. (9)

Down

1. And Christ _____ me too. (7)

4. The oil was worth a lot of _____. (5)

6. I had my bottle of sweet smelling _____. (3)

Comforter Puzzle Grid

Tender Hearted ~ John 19:38-42; 20:7; Matthew 27:60; Luke 23:50-55; Mark 15:42-45

Riddle: Christ had died. We buried him. Who are we?

Our Story: We were Christ's men. We had a job to do. Our holy day was soon. We had to get the body of Christ. Someone got a guard. He had to see if Christ was dead.

The guard said yes. He said we may have Christ's body.

My friend came with me to get Christ. He was taken down from the cross. My friend had a job too. He had many herbs and spices. We wrapped the body of Christ.

Tender Hearted ~ John 19:38-42; 20:7; Matthew 27:60; Luke 23:50-55; Mark 15:42-45

Bonus: Name my friend.

The body was in the spices and clean cloth.

We left where Christ had died. Women came too. My burying place was in a garden. It was a new cave. We put Christ's body in there. We put a cloth over his face.

The women saw what we did. We set the stone over the hole.

We were tender hearted. We loved Christ. He loved us all.

Tender Hearted Puzzle Clues

Across

4. We put a _____ over his face. (5)

5. He was taken down from the _____. (5)

Down

1. The body was in the _____ and clean cloth. (6)

2. Someone got the _____. (5)

3. We had a _____ to do. (3)

6. We set the _____ over the hole. (5)

Tender Hearted Puzzle Grid

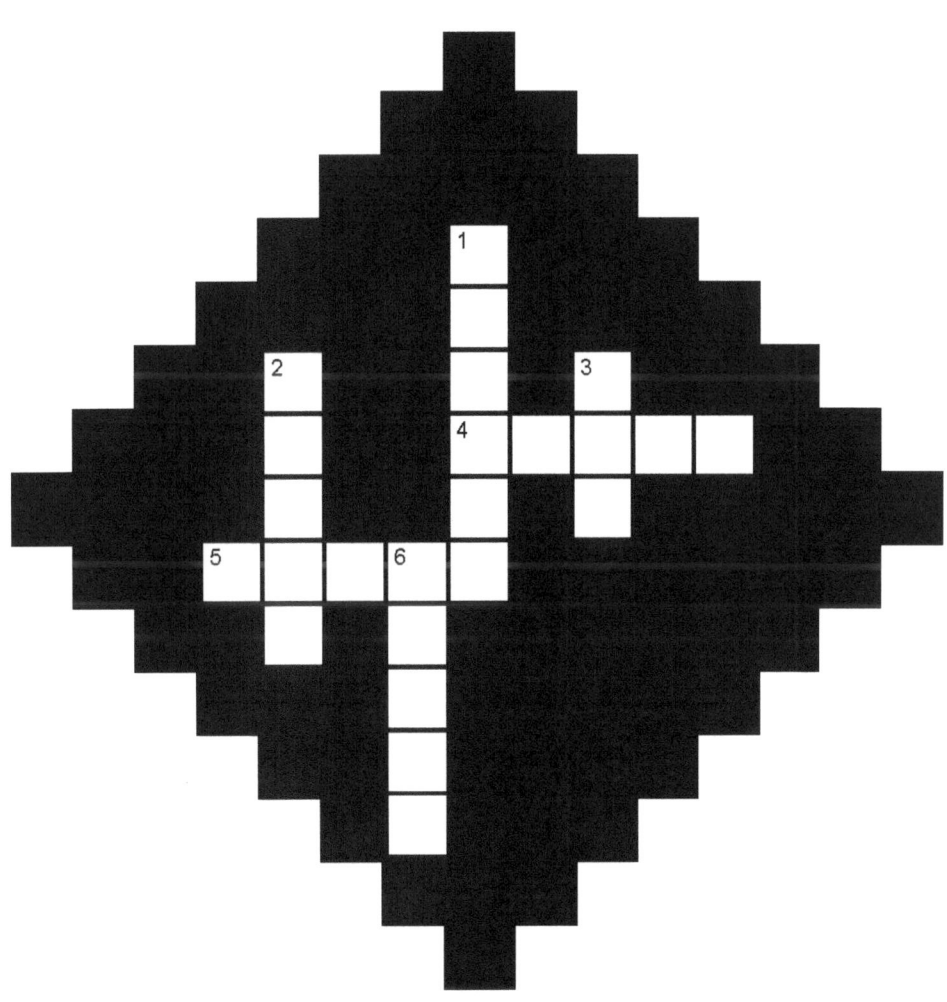

Trustworthy Women ~ Matthew 28:1-10

Riddle: Christ had died. We went to where he was buried. Who are we?

Our Story: We two women came to where Christ was buried. And the ground shook. An angel came down. He rolled back the stone door. The angel sat on the stone. He looked like lightning. His clothes were white as snow.

The angel said to not be sad. Christ had risen as he said. And yes. The cave was empty. He was not there. The angel said to tell Christ's men. That he is alive. And we will see him soon. We ran away in great joy.

81

Trustworthy Women ~ Matthew 28:1-10

Bonus: What were our names?

We met Christ on our way. He said, "All hail."

Our dear Christ was alive. We women bowed down. We lay our hands on his feet.

We worshiped him. He said, "Do not fear. Go tell my men. I will see them."

We obeyed Christ. We were trustworthy women.

Trustworthy Women Puzzle Clues

Across

3. Christ had _____ as he said. (5)

4. That he is _____. (5)

5. We women _____ down. (5)

6. What were our names? (4)

Down

1. We were _____ women. (11)

2. Who sat on the stone? (5)

Trustworthy Women Puzzle Grid

Bold Believers ~ Acts 3:1-10; 4:1-22

Riddle: I healed a man. My friend and I spoke about Christ. Who are we?

Our Story: A man's legs did not work. He begged us for money. I said, "In the name of Christ rise and walk."

I lifted him up. His feet became strong. His ankle bones were strong. The man walked. He was happy. We talked to the people about Christ. Many liked what we said.

Now the rulers were upset. They made us leave.

85

Bold Believers ~ Acts 3:1-10; 4:1-22

Bonus: Name the gate where the people were.

It was now the next day. The rulers asked by what name did we teach.

The Holy Ghost came over me. "We teach in the name of Christ. He rose from the dead. By Christ's name this man now walks. Christ is the only way to be saved."

The rulers said to not teach in the name of Christ. But we had to speak of the things we saw. We had to speak of the things we heard. The rulers let us go.

We believed in Christ. God blessed us when we believed. He made us bold.

Bold Believers Puzzle Clues

Across

2. Christ is the only way to be _____. (5)

3. His feet became _____. (6)

6. Now the _____ were upset. (6)

Down

1. Name the gate where the people were. (9)

4. The Holy _____ came over me. (5)

5. A man's _____ did not work. (4)

Bold Believers Puzzle Grid

Truth Seeker Acts 8:26-39

Riddle: I sat in my chariot. I wanted to know the Word of God. Who am I?

My Story: A man ran to me. The Spirit told him to come see me. The man wanted to know if I understood what I read. I needed someone to guide me. I asked the man to come sit beside me. And he did.

I read out loud about a man. It said the man was to die. He did not try to stop it. He was humble. His life will be taken from the earth.

I said, "Who was this that God talked about?" The man said it was about Christ.

89

Truth Seeker Acts 8:26-39

Bonus: Name the man who baptized me.

We came to a body of water. I said, "See the water. What keeps me from being baptized?" The man said I had to believe. With all my heart. I believed Christ is the Son of God.

The man dunked me under the water. I was being baptized. I came up out of the water. The Spirit of the Lord came. He took the man away.

I was a truth seeker. God blessed me. Now I follow Christ.

Truth Seeker Puzzle Clues

Across

2. Name the man who baptized me. (6)

3. The man told me it was about _____. (6)

4. I wanted to know the _____ of God. (4)

Down

1. I sat in my _____. (7)

5. The man _____ me under the water. (6)

Truth Seeker Puzzle Grid

Resilient ~ Acts 9:1-22

Riddle: I hurt people. Now I am blind. Who am I?

My Story: I went out to hurt the Lord's disciples. But a light came from heaven. A voice said my name. "Why do you bully me?" I asked who he was. He said, "I am Christ whom you bully." I asked him what he wanted. He said, "Go into the city. Someone will tell you." Men led me by my hands. I waited at Judas' house.

For three days I was blind. I did not eat or drink. Then a man came. He laid his hands on me. Christ told him that he chose me. The Holy Ghost will be with me.

Resilient ~ Acts 9:1-22

Bonus: Name the man who laid hands on me.

I saw again. The man dunked me under the water. I was baptized. I had a job. I was to tell people about Christ. And I will suffer for him.

I ate food. I became strong. Then I preached about Christ. I said he was God's Son. People were shocked. They knew I used to hurt his people. Now I proved to them he was the Christ.

I was resilient in a bad way. God helped me. Now I was resilient in a good way.

94

Resilient Puzzle Clues

Across

2. For three days I was _____. (5)

3. People were _____. (7)

5. But a _____ came from heaven. (5)

Down

1. Name the man who laid hands on me. (7)

2. Why do you _____ me? (5)

4. Then I preached about _____. (6)

Resilient Puzzle Grid

God's Servant ~ Acts 9:10-18

Riddle: The Lord wanted me to help a bad man. I did not want to. Who am I?

My Story: The Lord said my name. "I am here, Lord." He said, "Go to a certain street. Call on the house of Judas. Ask for Saul. He sees you in a vision. Put your hands on Saul's eyes. Then he will see again."

"But, Lord, many say he is evil. He has done bad things to your saints. He can still hurt all that call on your name." The Lord said, "Go as I have said. I chose him."

God's Servant ~ Acts 9:10-18

Bonus: Name the street where I found Saul.

The Lord said, "He will bring my name to the Gentiles. He will bring my name to kings. Even the children of Israel will hear him. Saul will suffer for me." I went on the street. I went into the house. I put my hands on Saul. "Brother Saul. Christ the Lord came to you. He sent me to you. You will see again. You will be full of the Holy Ghost."

Saul's eyes saw again. He rose. I baptized him. Saul did not hurt me. I was God's servant. And Saul did great things in the name of Christ.

God's Servant Puzzle Clues

Across

1. Ask for _____. (4)

2. I _____ him. (5)

3. I _____ him. (8)

4. He will bring my name to the _____. (8)

Down

1. I was God's _____. (7)

5. But, Lord, many say he is _____. (4)

God's Servant Puzzle Grid

Content ~ Acts 16:16-34; Philippians 4:11

Riddle: My friend and I were content. We were joyful in our pain. Who are we?

Our Story: I did a miracle. This made people mad. They took us to the rulers. Guards beat us. They put us into jail. The jailer put our feet in wooden locks. The wood hurt our feet. Our beaten backs hurt like bee stings.

We needed to be content in our cell. We prayed. We sang songs to God. It made us content. The other people in the jail listened to us.

Content ~ Acts 16:16-34; Philippians 4:11

Bonus: Name my friend.

Soon the floor of the cell shook. All the cell doors opened. The locks fell off of our feet.

The jailer ran to us. He was sure people got away. I said, "We are all here." The jailer came to our cell. He fell at our feet. "Sirs, what must I do to be saved?"

We said, "Believe in Christ the Lord. You will be saved, you and your kin."

The jailer washed our wounds. We baptized the jailer and his kin. The jailer trusted in Christ. God saved him and his kin. We were content. **102**

Content Puzzle Clues

Across

3. Sirs, what must I do to be _____? (5)

4. Name my friend. (5)

Down

1. The _____ hurt our feet. (4)

2. They put us into _____. (4)

4. We _____ songs to God. (4)

Content Puzzle Grid

Testifier ~ Revelation 1:1, 9-11, 20; 4:1-5; 7:11-17

Riddle: God put me on an island. I had much to hear. Who am I?

My Story: People needed God's words. God said, "Write what you see in a book."

I was to send this book to seven churches. Now a door opened in heaven. God said, "Come up. I will show things to come."

A throne was in heaven. A man sat on the throne. He was shiny like a stone. A rainbow was over the throne. People wore white robes. They had crowns of gold on their heads.

Testifier ~ Revelation 1:1, 9-11, 20; 4:1-5; 7:11-17

Bonus: Name the island.

Thunder came from the throne. The people bowed. The angels bowed. They said, "You are our God forever." The angel asked me who the people were. I said, "Sir, I do not know."

He said, "They came out of much sadness. But their robes are washed white in Christ. Now they serve God day and night. Christ will feed them. He will take them to waters. God will wipe away all their tears. I was a testifier. I told what I saw. Christ's people now see the hope to come.

Testifier Puzzle Clues

Across

2. Name the island. (6)

4. A _____ was over the throne. (7)

5. I was to send this book to _____ churches. (5)

Down

1. God put me on an_____. (6)

3. God will wipe away all their _____. (5)

4. But their _____ are washed white in Christ. (5)

Testifier Puzzle Grid

Listening

2. Plan

4. Faith

5. Tongue

6. Talked

1. Zacharias

3. Prophet

Joyful

1. Blessed

3. John

4. Mary

2. Son

3. Joy

Favored

3. Christ

6. Gabriel

1. Favored

2. Heart

4. Holy

5. Server

Obeying

3. Nazareth

5. Gifts

1. Four

2. Mary

4. Angel

6. Star

Self-Control

3. Camel

4. John

5. Baptized

1. Jordan

2. Dove

3. Christ

Patient

1. Christ

3. Gift

5. Blessed

6. Patient

2. Simeon

4. Temple

Faithful

2. Angels

4. Wilderness

6. Faithful

1. Devil

3. God

5. Eat

Perfect Love

3. Christ

5. Kingdom

6. Love

1. Disciples

2. Children

4. Truth

Thankful

3. King

4. Jerusalem

6. Crowd

1. Donkey

2. Limbs

5. Lord

109

Discernment

2. Christ
4. Angry
6. Evil
1. Animals
3. Temple
5. Good

Honesty

2. Done
3. Wise
4. Gift
1. Honesty
3. Waterpot

Sharing Lad

2. Faint
5. Basket
6. Lad
1. Christ
3. Twelve
4. Feed

Generous Stranger

1. Money
3. Priest
4. Jericho
5. Generous
6. Sad
2. Neighbors

Devotion

3. Mary
4. Christ
5. Good
1. Martha
2. Devotion

Truth Teller

3. Siloam
4. Son
5. Eyes
1. Bowed
2. Fish
3. Sinner

Vow Keeper

2. House
4. Sinner
5. Vow
1. Zacchaeus
3. Sycomore
4. Short

Believing Women

4. Lazarus
5. Brother
6. Feet
1. Christ
2. Believed
3. Dead

Compassion

3. Compassion
4. Bethany
5. Afraid
1. Glory
2. Martha
3. Cave

Comforter

2. Burial

3. Judas

5. Comforter

1. Blessed

4. Money

6. Oil

Tender Hearted

4. Cloth

5. Cross

1. Spices

2. Guard

3. Job

6. Stone

Trustworthy Women

3. Risen

4. Alive

5. Bowed

6. Mary

1. Trustworthy

2. Angel

Bold Believers

2. Saved

3. Strong

6. Rulers

1. Beautiful

4. Ghost

5. Legs

Truth Seeker

2. Philip

3. Christ

4. Word

1. Chariot

5. Dunked

Resilient

2. Blind

3. Shocked

5. Light

1. Ananias

2. Bully

4. Christ

God's Servant

1. Saul

2. Chose

3. Baptized

4. Gentiles

1. Servant

5. Evil

Content

3. Saved

4. Silas

1. Wood

2. Jail

4. Sang

Testifier

2. Patmos

4. Rainbow

5. Seven

1. Island

3. Tears

4. Robes

Jean Ann Williams lives on the Coast of Oregon with her husband Jim. She began her writing career in 1994 by reading a stack of books on the craft of writing. Since then, Jean Ann has published over 300 articles and short stories on the topics of Christianity, health, travel, friendships, relationships, family life, Sunday school take-home papers, and the loss of a child by suicide. Jean Ann's favorite animal is the goat. In her free time, she enjoys Crocheting, reading Inspirational books, gardening, and playing Scrabble with her grandchildren. Sometimes they let Nana win.

Author Website

www.jeanannwilliamsauthor.com

Contact the Author: jeanann_w@yahoo.com

Carley Herlihy is an illustrator known for her engaging and vibrant artwork that brings stories to life. Her journey in illustration began with collaborating with Jean Ann Williams on "27 Characters of the Old Testament: Stories & Activities for Children," where she skillfully combined creativity with educational themes. Carley has also designed some of Jean Ann Williams' captivating book covers, including the enchanting "Season of the Fawns." With a passion for storytelling and a keen eye for detail, her work continues to inspire readers of all ages.

Coming Winter 2027

Robert Sheffey Loved to Pray: And Eat A Lot Of Honey

www.ingramcontent.com/pod-product-compliance
Lightning Source LLC
Chambersburg PA
CBHW041548120626
46551CB00002B/152